Antipasti

Antipasti

First published in the UK in 2007 by
Apple Press
Sheridan House
114 Western Road
Hove
East Sussex
BN3 IDD
United Kingdom
www.apple-press.com

© Food Editore srl, 2005
Via Bordoni, 8 - 20124 MILANO
Via Mazzini, 6 - 43100 PARMA
www.gruppofood.com

Thanks to:
Alberto Rossi and Davide Di Prato (illustrations)
Simone Rugiati and Licia Cagnoni (recipes)
I Love My House, Barazzoni, Parma (the shop that provided the cooking utensils)
Sauro Antonioli (recipe on page 84)
Fabio Rossi (recipe on page 80)
Morgan Sella (recipe on page 24)

Printed in Croatia

ISBN 978-1-84543-186-0

Antipasti

Authentic Italian Recipes
for Every Occasion

APPLE

Contents

Basic techniques

THE TRADITION OF HORS D'OEUVRE

Usually served before lunch or dinner, as the name itself suggests, hors d'oeuvres are one of the most eclectic dishes in cuisine: they can be proposed for a cocktail or an appetizer, properly substitute first and second courses or a fresh vegetable side-dish and, why not, can be served as a main dish.

Small and quick hors d'oeuvre are particularly suited for buffet lunches or cocktails, where guests help themselves directly from serving plates; there are those who call them "fingerfood", others "tapas" or "mise en bouche", in any way, regardless of the name, the concept is always the same: mini pizzas, small quiches, vol-au-vent or rissoles to eat with your fingers.

Meat, fish, vegetarian, warm or cold, cooked or raw, this book presents a wide selection of hors d'oeuvre. Just one tip: Appetizers should be the lightest dish of the whole meal, so you'd better start with more delicate foods and finish with stronger ones – an ever-increasing intensity of tastes and flavours.

Hors d'oeuvre boast a long tradition in gastronomic culture: in their banquets, the Ancient Romans used to begin lunch with light and appetizing dishes, called «gustio» or «gustatio», served with mulsum, a wine and honey beverage; hard-boiled egg was the customary dish.

According to the historical period, hors d'oeuvre have had a different position in the dish sequence. Today, however, as a general rule they are served before soups. In the Italian gastronomic tradition, the number of appetizers has been considerably reduced to no more than two courses even on formal occasions.

The Italian appetizer par excellence includes "salumi" (different kinds of cold meat, usually made of pork), Parma ham and culatello of Zibello are among the classics. If "salumi" are sweet, you'd better serve them with salty bread; on the contrary, if they are tasty and spicy, you'd better choose bland bread, for example Tuscan bread. If you can, try to slice "salumi" by hand or using a manual slicing machine. Because of its high speed, an electric slicing machine tends to melt "salumi" fat that should melt in your mouth. Fish hors d'oeuvre are also very popular. From the traditional smoked salmon, served on buttered croutons, to anchovies, drained and rinsed, in oil or marinaded, and from seafood salad to raw fish carpaccio.

Moreover, regional cuisines offer many specialities, such as oil cakes, Palermitan croquettes seasoned with lemon, Piedmontese bagna cauda, fried olives of Ascoli, croutons with Tuscan chicken livers or Sicilian rice croquettes (arancini).

There are some countries where hors d'oeuvre are still very important, if not more important than any other dish served during lunch and dinner. For example, in the Scandinavian countries, notably Sweden, "smorgasbord", literally "board of bread", is a complete meal. You begin with different kinds of fish and crustaceans, go on with "salumi" and smoked meats then finish with warm dishes; the whole meal is served with different types of bread, including the characteristic rye crispbreads, salads and very strong alcoholic drinks.

The most famous appetizer however is the mix of Russian "zakouski", which includes "pirojiki" (puffs or stuffed puff pastry parcels), caviar and other fish roe, small pieces of rye bread with sauerkraut and smoked goose, potato and beet salads, and different kinds of smoked or marinaded fishes.

Another well-known mix of hors d'oeuvre are the "mezzes"; native to Lebanon, today they are widely spread all over the Middle East. This kind of appetizer reflects not only a gastronomic tradition but almost a way of understanding life. It consists of a series of small courses (from a minimum of four to a maximum of about forty), all served with a beverage made of dry anise distillate, called arak, that must be diluted with water and ice.

Chickpea purée (hummus), sesame seed purée (thaina), dried broad bean croquettes (falafel), rice rolls wrapped in grape leaves (dolmades), fried puff pastries stuffed with meat or cheese, fish roe sauce (taramosalada) or garlic, yoghurt and cucumber sauce (called tzaziki in Greece, cacik in Turkey) are only some examples of the most popular mezzes.

Mezzes represent an important opportunity for gathering together that, sometimes, can last many hours.

BASIC DOUGHS
Puff pastry

Puff pastry is the ideal "base" for many recipes. It's light and crumbly and it's suitable for preparing many different dishes, both sweet and salty.

Ingredients
200g/7oz/1 cup plain white flour
250g/9oz/1 cup margarine
100ml/3 ½fl oz/½ cup water
a pinch of salt

Preparation
Pour the flour into a pile, make a well in the middle then add water and salt.

When the dough has reached the right texture, wrap it with a kitchen cloth and leave to rest for about 20 minutes.

Using a rolling pin flatten the dough until you get a 5 mm/¼in thick square. Place the finely crumbled margarine in the middle, fold over the dough and close it completely, as to form a parcel. Flatten gently using a rolling pin, wrap the pastry in aluminium foil and allow to rest in the fridge for 5 minutes.

First "step": Place the dough again on the work top and roll it out into a long strip (about 1 cm/½in thick). Fold it up in three stages (fold one third towards the middle and cover it with the remaining third, to form three layers), then turn it around 90°.

Second "step": Roll the pastry out into a long strip, fold it up again in three stages, wrap in aluminium foil and keep in the fridge for approximately 30 minutes. Repeat these steps twice more, 6 "steps" in all.

After the last "step" leave the puff pastry to rest in the fridge for almost 1 hour, then use it as a base for your recipe.

The chef's secrets

To prepare a workman-like dough, it's very important that all the ingredients are the same temperature, so as to perfectly mix them. Margarine in particular must have the same temperature as pastry. If margarine is too cold, it could crumble the dough; on the other hand, if it is too warm, it could be runny.

Be careful not to substitute margarine with butter, as the latter contains very little water and, unlike margarine, it doesn't release steam that during baking swells the flour, allowing the pastry to rise well.

Remember to score the dough top making a small hole, so that steam can escape during baking without damping the pastry too much. If you want to nicely brown your dough, brush it with a lightly beaten egg or with milk before baking.

Cooking tips

Puff pastry is certainly one of the most versatile doughs, because it can be used to prepare both sweet and savoury recipes.

In our case, puff pastry turns out to be very useful to shape rolls or small baskets for mousses and savoury sauces, to prepare vol-au-vent, small pastry parcels stuffed with vegetables and bechamel or savoury pies.

It is also particularly suited to cover vegetable pies baked in the oven or to be thinly flattened and flavoured to make crumbly and crispy crackers.

Pâte brisée
Ingredients

300g/10½oz/2½ cups plain white flour
70g/2½oz/¼ cup margarine
1 egg
1 tbsp extra virgin olive oil
salt

Preparation

Pour flour, butter and salt into a pile. Make a well in the middle then add an egg, oil, salt and 100ml/4fl oz/½ cup lukewarm water.

Work the ingredients until you get a soft and elastic dough, wrap it in clingfilm and allow to rest in the fridge.

The chef's secrets

It's very important to use butter and eggs at room temperature and quickly work the dough so as not to excessively heat the butter, risking getting a dough which is not elastic enough. Allow the dough to rest in the fridge for at least 30 minutes, so that the ingredients can mix well.

If you use pâte brisée as a base for savoury pies, remember to prick the base with a fork to prevent it from swelling during baking and therefore

spoiling the pie. Pâte brisée can be kept in the fridge for a couple of days, wrapped in aluminium foil.
Alternatively, you may also deep-freeze it and slowly thaw it out before using.

Cooking tips

Pâte brisée is nothing less than savoury short pastry, so it's mainly used as a base for pies, tarts, small rolls and for many other different shapes to be filled and baked after brushing with beaten egg or milk.
You can prepare a much richer, crispier and unusual pâte brisée by simply dusting it with sesame, poppy or any other kind of seeds.

Savoury pastry rolls (cannoncini)

This is the usual recipe to make simple and tasty savoury "cannoncini" that can be stuffed with a variety of ingredients. These pastry rolls are very handy and simple as they can be prepared in advance and filled later.

Preparation

Stretch the pâte brisée on a work top. Using a cutting wheel or a sharp knife cut it into strips as large as the cylindrical steel moulds you'll use to give "cannoncini" their characteristic horn shape. Roll up the pate strips around the cylindrical moulds, leaving

2cm/¾in to close the pastry rolls. Brush this edge of the pate with little beaten white egg and thoroughly seal the "cannoncini".
Heat enough sunflower or other vegetable oil and, when hot, fry the pastry rolls (see below), then thoroughly drain them on kitchen paper.

The chef's secrets

Remove the pâte from its package and start kneading before its surface becomes dry and crumbles, or wrap it with a lightly dampened cloth in order to preserve it.
You may also use filo pastry for baked snacks or pastry crackers, rolled very thin, and served with fresh cheese and vegetable mousses.

Cooking tips

If you like, you can stuff "cannoncini" with ricotta cheese mixed with oil, oregano, salt and pepper then place a teaspoon of diced tomato pulp and fresh basil in the middle; or you may prefer stuffings prepared with white fish, such as grouper or cod, flavoured with aromatic herbs and lemon peel.

SAUCES

Sauces and mousses are particularly suited to stuff canapés, "bruschette" (toasts seasoned with olive oil and garlic) and salt puffs or to dip vegetables of a fresh pinzimonio salad. You'll find out that these "basic" sauces are precious allies, as they improve tastes and flavours.

Ricotta cheese sauce with ginger and chives
Ingredients
200g/7oz/1 cup fresh ricotta cheese
fresh chives, chopped
20g/¾oz/1 tbsp fresh ginger
1 tbsp extra virgin olive oil
salt and pepper

Preparation
Pass ricotta cheese through a sieve, then work it using a spatula until you get a soft, smooth cream without lumps; season it with extra virgin olive oil, salt and pepper. Grate the ginger root and gently squeeze its pulp in your hands until the juice drops fall into the sauce. Add chives and leave ricotta cheese to rest in the fridge for 1 hour, then serve.

Yoghurt sauce
Ingredients
2 tbsp fresh herbs, chopped
(parsley, dill, oregano, basil)
400ml/14fl oz/1¾ cups Greek yoghurt
2 cloves of garlic
2 tbsp honey
1 tsp salt
black pepper

Preparation
Mix all the ingredients in a bowl, until you get a smooth

mixture without lumps.
Pass yoghurt sauce through a sieve to remove any lumps.
Allow to rest in the fridge over night.
You may serve this sauce together with mixed seasonal vegetables or salad.

Salmon sauce
Ingredients
80g/3oz smoked salmon
1 white onion
200g/7oz/1 cup robiola cheese
½ tsp paprika
salt

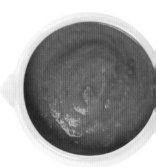

Preparation
Thinly chop onion and salmon and mix them with robiola cheese; season with paprika and salt.
Allow the sauce to rest in the fridge for 1 hour, then stuff tarts or vol-au-vent.

Ham mousse
Ingredients
450g/1lb/2 cups cooked ham, diced
    or cut into strips
70g/2½oz/¼ cup butter
1 glass of milk
20g/¾oz/1½ tbsp plain white flour
200ml/7fl oz/¾ cup fresh cream
nutmeg
salt and pepper

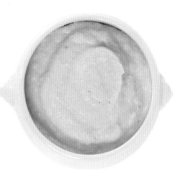

Preparation

Process cooked ham in a food processor.

In a saucepan melt 20 g/¾ oz/1 tbsp of butter, remove from the heat and pour in the flour. Stir constantly, then place the saucepan again over a low heat.

Gradually pour in milk and boil for 3 minutes; add salt and pepper then dust with nutmeg.

Combine ham and bechamel sauce, then pass the mixture through a sieve. Whip up the cream, work the remaining butter until soft, then combine these 2 ingredients with ham-bechamel sauce mixture.

Put ham mousse in a buttered mould and allow it to rest in the fridge for 3-4 hours. You may like to spread this delicate mousse on crackers or on your favourite bread, even flavoured bread.

Whisked mustard
Ingredients
1 egg yolk
1 tbsp sweet mustard
1 tbsp balsamic vinegar
8 tbsp sunflower oil
1 tbsp extra virgin olive oil
salt and pepper

Preparation

In a bowl beat the egg yolk and sweet mustard, then gradually pour in balsamic vinegar. Add seed oil and olive oil, being careful to stir constantly to avoid splitting mayonnaise. Season to taste with salt and pepper. This sauce is particularly suited to dip raw vegetables and it's also the best alternative to butter for preparing smoked fish croutons.

Hollandaise sauce
Ingredients
2 egg yolks
100g/3½oz/½ cup butter
1 tbsp plain white flour
1 tbsp stock
200ml/7fl oz/1 cup vinegar
salt and pepper

Preparation

Boil vinegar with salt and pepper, until reduced to about half then, as soon as tepid, pour in 1 tablespoon of stock, add the egg yolks and 50g/1¾oz/¼ cup of crumbled butter.

In a saucepan, in a bain-marie, gently beat the mixture using a whisk and, while mixing the ingredients, add the remaining butter, the flour and a little cold water.

To remove any lumps, pass the mixture through a sieve and be careful to keep it in a bain-marie until you're ready to serve.

HORS D'OEUVRE PRESENTATION
Hors d'oeuvre are the first dish to be served and their purpose is to whet the appetite for what will come next.

Hors d'oeuvre however don't only play a gastronomical role. Colours should strike the eye, smells should seduce and tastes should awaken imagination. This is why plate arrangement requires great attention; at least as much attention as you pay to food preparation.

Most important in presenting hors d'oeuvre is to offer

them in small and appetizing portions that your guests will devour with their eyes and be tempted by. Etiquette suggests serving appetizers on small plates that can be easily filled and at the same time give the impression of being generous.

According to etiquette, canapés and croutons should be served on separate trays so that guests can help themselves with their fingers; olives should be served in a small bowl together with a spoon, while sardines and caviar on a plate with a slice of toast. Pâté should be presented on a plate with a spatula.

Pies and timbales look much more attractive if served in single portions on a bed of vegetables or aromatic herbs together with a coloured and scented sauce; creams and pâté are really appetizing if presented on canapés or croutons in soft and light flakes, obtained using a pastry bag (sac-à-poche), or arranged in cups and bowls with fruits or vegetables.

With regard to "salumi" presentation, remember that they are particularly suited to be rolled on breadsticks and on vegetable julienne strips or to be stuffed with various fillings.

Moreover, hors d'oeuvre are very handy because you can prepare most of them in advance.

Terrines and pâté will turn out much tastier if prepared the day before, the same is also true for creams and sauces; in this case you'd better remove them from the fridge at least 30 minutes before serving.

Savoury pies, quiches and tarts can be heated up a couple of minutes before serving.

This brief introduction is a reminder that it is often possible to serve high quality dishes without too much stress.

Meat, cheese and vegetables

Savoury and original ideas to whet the appetite with tasty meat, cold meat and cheese appetizers or with light vegetable courses.

Light caponata with puff pastry vegetables

Serves 4

Caponata

8 small courgettes
½ yellow pepper
½ red pepper
8 cherry tomatoes
200g/7oz/1 cup pumpkin
½ white onion, coarsely chopped
8 tbsp extra virgin olive oil
1 clove garlic
oregano
salt and pepper

Puff pastry

1 puff pastry roll

Preparation time: 20 minutes
Cooking time: 40 minutes
Difficulty: easy
Wine: Montecarlo Bianco

Wash courgettes, tomatoes and peppers, then dice them. Peel the pumpkin and cut it into medium to small cubes. In a saucepan heat the oil with an unpeeled garlic clove, then add the onion.

After 3 minutes add diced pumpkin and then the peppers. Slightly salt and cook for 6-7 minutes pouring in a little water, if necessary. Add courgettes and tomatoes, sprinkle with oregano and a little pepper, then finish cooking.

Meanwhile, cut puff pastry into 4 rings (6cm/2½in each), arrange them on 4 semispherical moulds and bake at 200°C/400°F/Gas 6 for 10 minutes. When ready, take puff pastry out of the oven and use it to serve hot vegetable caponata.

"Polentine" fancies (small pieces of polenta)

Serves 4

Fancies

250g/9oz/1 cup instant polenta flour
1 carrot
1 courgette
1 stalk of celery
2 tbsp Taggiasche olives in oil
3 tbsp tomato pulp
1 porcino mushroom
1 clove garlic
6 tbsp extra virgin olive oil
thyme, oregano
salt and pepper

Preparation time: 35 minutes
Cooking time: 25 minutes
Difficulty: easy
Wine: Rossese di Dolceacqua

Peel the carrot and the courgette. Chop the carrot, the celery and the courgette, then sauté with a drizzle of oil for 2 minutes.

To prepare the polenta, bring to the boil some salted water with 2 tablespoons of oil, then gradually pour in the flour stirring with a whisk. When it's still soft, pour ¾ of it into a plastic rectangular mould to a thickness of 5mm/¼in, then combine sautéed vegetables with the remaining polenta. In a small saucepan sauté Taggiasche olives with a little oil, tomato and fresh oregano.

Thoroughly clean the porcino mushroom, dice it and cook in a saucepan with oil, crushed garlic, thyme, salt and pepper. Cut cold polenta using a circular and a triangular pasta cutter, then fry the little triangles that you'll serve with olive and tomato sauce. Quickly cook polenta rings in a non-stick pan and serve with sautéed mushrooms.

Using an ice-cream scoop make 4 spheres from the polenta with vegetables. Arrange the dish and serve.

Vegetable sushi

Serves 4

Sushi
4 sheets of alga nori
150g/5oz/1 cup white Basmati rice
5cm/2in alga kombu
2 tbsp tahin
2 tbsp rice vinegar
1 tsp sugar
1 tbsp rice oil
1 carrot
1 courgette
1 heart of red chicory

Preparation time: 20 minutes
Cooking time: 12 minutes
Difficulty: easy
Wine: Prosecco di Conegliano
e Valdobbiadene Brut

Cook the rice with a piece of kombu alga for 12 minutes; meanwhile dissolve the sugar in the rice vinegar. Remove kombu alga, let the rice swell up then stir in the rice vinegar. Add a tablespoon of rice oil and leave to rest for 10 minutes.

Toast alga nori on a high heat. With wet hands, spread the rice on the alga, brush it with tahin and arrange the vegetables cut into very thin sticks on it. Roll up using a bamboo mat. Damp the edge on the alga with a little cold water to seal it up.

Allow to rest in the fridge for 30 minutes and serve vegetable sushi cut into slices.

Spring onions with "cirighin" sauce

Serves 4

Spring onions
24 tender spring onions
200g/7oz/1 cup butter
100g/3½oz/½ cup Parmesan cheese, grated

Cirighin sauce
100ml/3½fl oz/½ cup chicken stock
4 eggs
Parmesan cheese, grated
salt

To garnish
½ Duia salami
extra virgin olive oil

Preparation time: 15 minutes
Cooking time: 10 minutes
Difficulty: easy
Wine: Alto Adige Sauvignon

Peel spring onions, boil them in salted water, drain and sauté with butter (see photo 1); sprinkle with plenty of Parmesan cheese and cook them "au gratin".

In an iron saucepan fry 4 eggs for "cirighin" (fried egg, see photo 2), add salt and process them in a food processor with the stock and a handful of Parmesan cheese. In another saucepan brown Duia salami with a drizzle of oil (see photo 3). Arrange spring onions on a plate, salt them and garnish with sautéed Duia salami.

Note - Duia salami is a Piedmontese speciality, made of pure pork, weighing about 200g/7oz. Its name comes from the peculiar method with which this salami is preserved: it is dipped in an earthenware vessel (duia), full of melted lard. Once hardened, the lard keeps the salami soft for several months. This preservation method also increases the hot taste of the salami.

Panzerotto with leek, bread and truffle

Serves 4

Pastry

150g/5oz/1 cup plain white flour
3½ tbsp water
3 tbsp extra virgin olive oil
1 tsp lard
salt

Stuffing

1 small leek
1 knob of butter
100g/3½oz wholemeal bread
1 white truffle
1 tbsp truffle oil
200ml/7fl oz/1 cup milk
oil for deep-frying
salt and pepper

Preparation time: 25 minutes
Cooking time: 15 minutes
Difficulty: easy
Wine: Dolcetto d'Alba

Pour the flour into a bowl and add oil, salt, water and lard; work the ingredients energically, then place them onto a work top kneading till you get a smooth and elastic ball. Leave to rest in the fridge wrapped in clingfilm.

Thoroughly wash the leek and cut it into thin round slices, then cook them in a saucepan with butter and a little water, if necessary, until rather transparent. Soak bread slices in milk and squeeze. Combine them with leek and flavour with truffle oil.

Warm the mixture and add ½ thinly chopped truffle; season to taste with salt and pepper.

Flatten puff pastry and cut it into big "cappellacci" (lengthened purses) and stuff them with the leek-bread mixture. Seal the edges and fry them in very hot oil. Cut warm panzerotti into slices and serve them with the remaining truffle.

Tarte tatin with courgettes and pecorino cheese

Serves 4

Tarte tatin

250g/9oz puff pastry
3 courgettes
150g/5oz/1 cup soft sweet pecorino cheese
2 tbsp almonds chopped
1 tbsp extra virgin olive oil
1 clove of garlic
1 bunch of parsley
4 tbsp corn oil
salt and pepper

Preparation time: 20 minutes
Cooking time: 35 minutes
Difficulty: easy
Wine: Roero Arneis

Crush the garlic by hand and quickly brown it in hot olive oil, then remove and add the parsley and courgettes cut into small pieces. Sauté them on a high heat for 5 minutes. Season to taste with salt and pepper.

Brush some little moulds with corn oil. Spread the bottom of the mould with almonds. Cook the courgettes with garlic and parsley, and add them with some flakes of pecorino cheese.

Cut puff pastry into 4 rings of the same diameter as the moulds. Arrange them over the filling and press gently to seal. Bake at 190°C/375°F/Gas 5 for 15 minutes.

Take the tarte tatin out of the oven and turn upside-down before serving.

Pork, Savoy cabbage and carrot terrine with cooked must

Serves 4

Pork
400g/14oz/1½ cup minced pork meat
3 carrots
120g/4oz/½ cup soft salami, diced
2 tbsp raisins
½ wine glass of Marsala
4 leaves of Savoy cabbage heart
3 tbsp extra virgin olive oil
salt and black pepper

To garnish
100 ml/3½fl oz/½ cup cooked grape
must

Preparation time: 20 minutes
Cooking time: 50 minutes
Difficulty: medium
Wine: Nebbiolo d'Alba

Soak raisins in Marsala wine. Blanch Savoy cabbage leaves in salted water and leave them to cool down on a cloth.

Peel the carrots, steam or boil them, then cut into thin slices and set aside.

Season the meat with salt, pepper, salami, oil and squeezed raisins. Line a terrine mould with greaseproof paper and fill it with meat alternated with vegetables. Press and cook in a bain-marie at 190°C/375 °F for 20 minutes with a weight on top.

Leave to rest for a few minutes and serve the terrine slices with grape must, thickened for 5 minutes on a low heat.

Pork loaf flavoured with Vernaccia of S. Gimignano

Serves 4

Pork loaf
400g/14oz cup pork shoulder or neck
500ml/18fl oz/2¼ cups Vernaccia of S. Gimignano
1litre/4 cups water
2 sticks of celery
1 carrot
1 red onion
2 leaves of laurel
4 leaves of sage
1 sprigs of rosemary
5 juniper berries
cooking salt

Haricot bean cream
200g/7oz/1 cup haricot beans
3 cloves of garlic
2 tbsp extra virgin olive oil
sage
ground black pepper
cooking salt

To garnish
1 yellow onion
oil for deep-frying

Preparation time: 25 minutes
Cooking time: 60 minutes
Difficulty: easy
Wine: Rubino di Cantavenna

Put all the chopped herbs and vegetables in a saucepan with water and bring to the boil with cooking salt; pour in wine, then add the pork. Simmer for about 30 minutes, turn off and leave the pork to cool down in its liquor.

Cook haricot beans in salted water with 3 cloves of unpeeled garlic; remove the garlic, drain the beans and process the beans with oil, sage, salt and pepper, until you get a smooth cream.

Arrange dallops of legume cream on the dishes and complete with some pork loaf crumbled by hand.

Garnish with onion rings fried in oil for deep-frying.

Cook's tip - If you want to make your pork loaf much richer, choose a red wine of middle structure such as the Nobile di Montepulciano.

Spicy lentil pâté

Serves 4

Pâté
200g/7oz/1 cup dried lentils
120g/4oz/1 cup chopped celery, carrot and onion
1 clove of garlic
500ml/18fl oz/2¼ cups vegetable stock
1 tsp tomato concentrate
1 tbsp parsley
6 tbsp extra virgin olive oil
1 tsp curry powder
salt and pepper

Preparation time: 30 minutes
Cooking time: 35 minutes
Difficulty: easy
Wine: Sorni Rosso

Rinse the lentils and soak them in cold water for about 2 hours.

Sauté chopped vegetables in a saucepan with olive oil and a garlic clove; add the lentils, 1 teaspoon of curry powder and tomato concentrate.

Leave to flavour for a couple of minutes, pour in hot stock and cook for 30 minutes; lentils should be soft and dry. Process them in a food processor until you get a thick purée, then season to taste with salt and pepper; add chopped parsley and mix well.

Divide the pâté into small cups and leave to cool down at room temperature.

Cook's tip - You may like to garnish with a few chervil or parsley leaves and serve the pâté with toasted bread croutons.

Tricolour vegetable jelly

Serves 4

Jelly
4 carrots
200g/7oz/1 cup spinach
200g/7oz/1 cup potatoes
2 tsp agar agar powder
1 sprig of thyme
salt

Preparation time: 40 minutes
Cooking time: 35 minutes
Difficulty: easy
Wine: Gambellara

Cook unpeeled potatoes; peel and mash them in a large bowl using a potato masher and season with thyme and salt. Liquidize the carrots, pour their juice into a small saucepan with 1 teaspoon of agar agar powder and cook on a low heat for 5 minutes. Leave to cool slightly.

Briefly blanch the spinach, then put it through a food processor. Pour spinach juice into another saucepan. Combine with the remaining agar agar powder and cook for 5 minutes.

Cool the green jelly too. Line a mould with clingfilm and compose the jelly arranging the carrot mixture first, spinach mixture next, then complete with potato purée.

Leave to cool in the fridge for 1 hour before serving.

SPINACH
As everybody knows, spinach is rich in iron, however it also contains vitamins (A and C). The best fresh spinach is tender and has crisp leaves.

Ravioli of pepper jelly and marinaded avocado

Serves 4

Ravioli
3 peppers (yellow, red, green)
a pinch of agar agar powder
6 tbsp extra virgin olive oil
100ml/3½fl oz/½ cup light vegetable stock
a pinch of sugar, salt

Filling
¼ cauliflower
2 tbsp fruity extra virgin olive oil
salt

Focaccia
200g/7oz/1 cup pizza dough
1 white onion
2 tbsp extra virgin olive oil, salt

Avocado
1 ripe avocado
fresh ginger
2 tbsp extra virgin olive oil
salt and white pepper

Preparation time: 35 minutes
Cooking time: 50 minutes
Difficulty: difficult
Wine: Sicilia Chardonnay

Clean peppers, discarding their seeds and pith. Peel them using a potato peeler, then dice separating them by colour. Cook peppers in 3 different saucepans with oil on a low heat. Melt the agar agar powder in hot vegetable stock and pour ⅓ in each pot. Process the 3 mixtures separately in a food processor, adding salt and a pinch of sugar to the green pepper (leave the mixtures rather liquid). Pour the mixture into round latex moulds or the bottom of plastic coffee glasses. Put in the fridge to thicken.

Meanwhile, roll out the dough on an oiled baking sheet; peel and slice the onion.

Sprinkle onion slices on the focaccia dough, season with salt and a drizzle of oil. Leave to rise again in a warm place, and bake at 220°C/425°F/Gas 7 for 35 minutes.

Wash the cauliflower and keep only the florets; process in a food processor. Season with salt and a drizzle of oil. Peel and dice the avocado, add oil and grated ginger, then season to taste with salt and white pepper. Remove the pepper jelly discs from their moulds and arrange them on plates, covering them with the cauliflower. Cover the cauliflower with a disc of a different colour and complete with the avocado.

Serve together with warm onion focaccia.

Potato and rocket terrine flavoured with thyme

Serves 4

Terrine
4 large yellow potatoes
1 bunch of rocket
2 slices of home-made bread
80g/3oz/¼ cup Parma ham, finely diced
1 sprig of thyme, chopped
4 tbsp extra virgin olive oil
1 clove of garlic
1 shallot, chopped
salt and pepper

Preparation time: 30 minutes
Cooking time: 30 minutes
Difficulty: easy
Wine: Malvasia Istriana

Place unpeeled potatoes in a saucepan full of cold salted water, bring to the boil and cook potatoes. When ready, leave to cool slightly, then peel the potatoes and mash them. Meanwhile, wash the rocket.

In a saucepan brown the shallot quickly in 2 tablespoons of oil, then add mashed potatoes, thyme and Parma ham. Leave to heat for 5 minutes.

When slightly cool, season to taste with salt and pepper. Add chopped rocket and place the mixture in a mould lined with clingfilm. Allow to rest in the fridge for 1 hour.

Pour the remaining oil into a non-stick pan, brown the garlic clove, then remove it. Toast small pieces of bread, then crumble them.

Remove the terrine from the mould, cover it with garlic-flavoured breadcrums, then serve the terrine sliced.

Rabbit and peppers

Serves 4

Rabbit
½ rabbit
½ yellow pepper
2 precooked tortillas
1 egg yolk
2 slices of bread
200ml/7fl oz/1 cup of milk
6 tbsp extra virgin olive oil
2 cloves of garlic
100ml/3½fl oz/½ cup chicken stock
½ wine glass of white wine
sprig each of sage, rosemary
salt and pepper

Salad
1 salad tomato
1 small bunch of mixed salad
balsamic vinegar

To garnish
½ red pepper

Preparation time: 45 minutes
Cooking time: 40 minutes
Difficulty: medium
Wine: Refosco dal Peduncolo Rosso

Cut the rabbit into several pieces and thoroughly wash it; quickly sauté the garlic in oil and brown the meat. Add sage and rosemary, then remove them halfway through the cooking. As soon as meat is lightly browned, pour in wine, salt and pepper. Cook until the alcohol is evaporated, peel the yellow pepper, cut it into 1cm/½in pieces and add. Cover and gently cook adding a little hot stock. Meanwhile, roast the red pepper and put it in a plastic bag to "sweat". Cut tortillas in a diamond shape and bake in pudding moulds at 200°C/400°F/Gas 6 for 5 minutes. Wash all the vegetables and prepare a salad.

Leave the rabbit to cool slightly, bone it and place in a food processor together with its juices, the cooked yellow pepper, egg yolk and bread soaked in milk and well squeezed. Mix and put in a sac-à-poche.

Arrange the salad on plates and season it with balsamic vinegar, then put the tortillas on top.

Roast red pepper on a high heat, put it into a plastic bag and leave to "sweat" for 20 minutes. Peel, wash and cut it into thin dices. Fill with rabbit mixture and garnish with red pepper. Serve tepid.

Ricotta cheese purses with diced tomatoes

Serves 4

Purses

4 filo pastry sheets
200g/7oz/1 cup sheep ricotta cheese
2 sprigs of thyme
1 tbsp Roman pecorino cheese
oil for deep-frying
ground black pepper

Tomatoes

2 San Marzano tomatoes, diced
1 clove of garlic
2 tbsp extra virgin olive oil
salt and pepper

Preparation time: 20 minutes
Cooking time: 5 minutes
Difficulty: easy
Wine: Bianco d'Alcamo

Stir ricotta cheese with pecorino cheese and thyme leaves until creamy. Add black pepper freshly ground. Divide filo pastry sheets and cut them into strips (8cm/3¼in wide).

Starting from the outside edge, place 1 teaspoon of ricotta mixture on the pastry and fold over three times, giving the pastry the shape of a purse. Repeat this for each strip using all the available mixture.

Season the tomatoes with garlic, oil, salt and pepper. Allow them to rest for 10 minutes. Heat the oil and fry the pastry purses. Serve them hot on diced tomatoes.

Cook's tip - Instead of filo pastry, you may use a very thin dough prepared with 100g/3½ oz/¾ cup of wheat flour and 100g/3½ oz/¾ cup of spelt flour. Add a pinch of salt and pepper, 1 tablespoon of extra virgin olive oil and lukewarm water to knead. Leave the dough to rest, stretch it until thin and go on as indicated in the recipe.

Chickpea and aubergine pâté

Serves 4

Pâté

200g/7oz/1 cup dried chickpeas
2 large aubergines
3 tbsp extra virgin olive oil
1 bunch of parsley, chopped
1 tbsp sesame oil
1 clove garlic
1 leaf of laurel
salt and pepper

To garnish

1 red pepper
1 yellow pepper
4 slices of bread (for croutons)

Preparation time: 15 minutes
Cooking time: 30 minutes
Difficulty: easy
Wine: Lacryma Christi Bianco

Soak the chickpeas in cold water for 12 hours, then blanch them with the laurel leaf and garlic clove.

Cut the aubergines in half lengthwise and score them with many parallel cuts; bake in oven at 180°C/350°F/Gas 4 for about 30 minutes until their pulp is tender. Using a spoon remove the pulp and process it with the blanched and drained chickpeas. Pass this mixture through a sieve, then into a bowl.

Season with extra virgin olive oil, sesame oil, parsley, salt and pepper. Keep in a cool place.

Roast peppers on a high heat, put them into a plastic bag and leave to "sweat" for 20 minutes. Peel, wash and cut them into thin julienne strips.

Arrange the aubergine and chickpea pâté in small dishes or single bowls, garnish with pepper julienne and serve with bread croutons, toasted in a non-stick pan or under the oven grill. Serve immediately.

Soft-boiled egg with green sauce

Serves 4

Egg
5 large fresh eggs
1 tbsp pine nuts
1 bunch of basil
6 tbsp extra virgin olive oil
parsley
salt and pepper

To garnish
½ black truffle

Preparation time: 10 minutes
Cooking time: 15 minutes
Difficulty: easy
Wine: Tocai Friulano

Break 4 eggs into 4 coffee cups and set aside, covering with clingfilm.

Prepare a hard-boiled egg. Meanwhile, thoroughly wash the basil and parsley under cold water and dry well; toast the pine nuts in a non-stick pan. Put basil, parsley and pine nuts in a food processor together with the hard-boiled egg white, oil, salt and pepper. Mix well until you get a creamy sauce (like pesto).

Heat a little water in a saucepan with a vegetable steamer; as soon as it boils, put the 4 coffee cups with eggs into the basket, cover and cook for about 9 minutes, until the eggs are boiled.

Pass the blade of a thin knife between the egg and the coffee cup, then place the eggs onto plates with green sauce. You may serve with truffle flakes.

FRESH EGGS
The flotation test is a safe method to evaluate egg freshness: dip the egg in a glass of salted water (10g/¼oz/½ tbsp of salt per 100ml/3½fl oz/½ cup of water). If it sinks, the egg is very fresh; if it remains halfway, the egg may be 6 days old; if it just surfaces, it's 11 days old and if it floats, you'd better throw it away.

Crispy polenta with pea cream

Serves 4

Polenta
100g/3½oz/¾ cup maize flour
300ml/10fl oz/1¼ cups water
oil for deep-frying
cooking salt

Pea cream
2 tbsp extra virgin olive oil
200g/7oz/1 cup fresh peas
1 shallot, finely chopped
100ml/3½fl oz/½ cup vegetable stock
½ chilli
chives
salt and pepper

Preparation time: 20 minutes
Cooking time: 55 minutes
Difficulty: easy
Wine: Gutturnio Classico

Boil the water with a pinch of cooking salt, then gradually pour in the maize flour. Leave it to thicken, then spoon the polenta into a square mould and allow it to cool.

Brown the shallot in a saucepan on a low heat with oil and chilli. Add peas and vegetable stock. When ready, season to taste with salt and pepper, then process the mixture in a food processor. Flavour with chives.

Dice the polenta and fry it in hot oil. Serve the crispy polenta with pea cream.

Mediterranean tapas with Parmesan cheese

Serves 4

Tapas
4 tbsp Parmesan cheese, grated
½ Golden apple
1 fillet of roasted red pepper
1 fillet of roasted yellow pepper
2 anchovy fillets in oil
2 tsp fresh caprino cheese (Italian goat's cheese)
1 knob of butter
chives
salt and pepper

Preparation time: 15 minutes
Cooking time: 20 minutes
Difficulty: medium
Wine: Cirò Bianco

Put a small non-stick pan on the cooker and place a round pasta cutter in the middle (4cm/1½in diameter). Pour 1 tablespoon of Parmesan cheese into the pasta cutter then, once shaped, remove the mould.

When nicely browned arrange the Parmesan waffle over a coffee cup and let it dry. Repeat this step 4 times.

Meanwhile, peel the peppers and cut them into small strips. Cut the apple into 1cm/½in cubes and sauté in a saucepan with butter, salt and pepper.

Arrange the apple in the middle of the waffle and garnish with pepper strips around. Put caprino cheese over the apple and complete with an anchovy fillet.

Dust with chives and serve.

Truffled mushroom pâté

Serves 4

Pâté

500g/1lb 2oz/2 cups mixed mushrooms
(porcini, champignon, honey mushrooms)
1 small onion
2 cloves of garlic
1 bunch of mixed herbs
(thyme, marjoram, chives)
100ml/3½fl oz/½ cup fresh cream
100g/3½oz/½ cup truffle butter
3 tbsp extra virgin olive oil
salt and pepper

To garnish

1 French loaf

Preparation time: 15 minutes
Cooking time: 25 minutes
Difficulty: easy
Wine: Rossese di Dolce Acqua

Thinly slice the onion and cook with oil and crushed garlic in a saucepan. Wash and slice mushrooms, add them, and cook for 15-20 minutes, stirring often.

Season to taste with salt and pepper, then remove the garlic and leave to cool slightly. Process the mixture adding cream and melted butter. Combine with chopped herbs, salt and pepper and pour the pâté into a bowl. Place in the fridge to thicken. Serve the pâté in single cups together with croutons of toasted bread. You may also shape some quenelle using 2 spoons, arrange them on a plate and serve with mixed salad.

Cook's tip - To preserve aromatic herbs, follow this simple procedure: chop the herbs, dividing them by type (see photo 1); put them in an ice tray, adding a little water (see photo 2). Deep-freeze in a freezer and, once the cubes are solidified, wrap them in tin foil (see photo 3), indicating with a felt-tip the corresponding herb. Keep in the freezer.

1

2

3

Steamed vegetables with yoghurt mayonnaise

Serves 6

Vegetables
3 carrots
2 yellow potatoes
2 cooked beetroots
2 courgettes

Sauce
1 carton of whole natural yoghurt
1 egg yolk
1 tsp lemon juice
a pinch of sweet mustard
100ml/3fl oz/½ cup corn oil
1 tsp chives, finely chopped
salt

Preparation time: 30 minutes
Cooking time: 15 minutes
Difficulty: easy
Wine: no wine recommended

Wash, peel and dice vegetables. Steam them using the proper basket.

Prepare the mayonnaise, whisking the egg yolk with salt, mustard and lemon juice. Go on mixing the egg yolk using a whisk or a hand mixer, pouring in corn oil. Add the yoghurt and fresh chives. Leave in the fridge for at least 2 hours before serving.

Serve vegetables together with yoghurt mayonnaise.

Cook's tip - Yoghurt mayonnaise is particularly suited to season mixed summer salads.

Courgettes stuffed with crispy marrow flowers

Serves 4

Courgettes
4 large courgettes

Stuffing
10 black olives
6 capers
1 bunch of basil
2 tbsp breadcrumbs
1 egg
2 cloves of garlic
a pinch of chilli
2 tbsp extra virgin olive oil

Marrow flowers
8 marrow flowers
50g/2oz/¼ cup plain white flour
very cold sparkling water
1 tbsp poppy seeds
oil for deep-frying
salt

Preparation time: 25 minutes
Cooking time: 25 minutes
Difficulty: easy
Wine: Terre di Franciacorta Bianco

In a large saucepan put chopped garlic with chilli and oil. Wash the courgettes and cut away their tips, then use a corer to remove the inner part.

Thinly cut courgette pulp and combine with garlic. Add capers, olives and crumbled basil. Cook on a high heat for 10 minutes adding, if necessary, 1 tablespoon of water. Remove the garlic and process in a food processor together with breadcrumbs and egg. Steam courgettes for 5 minutes, then stuff them with the filling. Bake at 180°C/350°F/Gas 4 for 10 minutes.

Meanwhile, heat oil to fry the marrow flowers. Prepare the batter with cold sparkling water, flour, poppy seeds and a pinch of salt. Dip the flowers, remove the excess batter and fry them. Serve stuffed courgettes and fried flowers immediately.

Cook's tip - To get a crispier fry, use very cold beer instead of sparkling water.

Small pastry cases with artichoke paste

Serves 4

Small pastry cases
4 filo pastry sheets
4 artichokes
1 shallot
40g/1½oz/3 tbsp cashew nuts, chopped
20g/¾oz/1 tbsp butter
a small piece of fresh sweet chilli
1 lemon
100ml/3½fl oz/½ cup vegetable stock
3 tbsp extra virgin olive oil
chives
parsley, chopped
salt and pepper

Preparation time: 20 minutes
Cooking time: 25 minutes
Difficulty: easy
Wine: Mlavasia Istriana

Divide filo pastry sheets and butter some moulds to be used in oven. Line them with filo pastry rings and bake at 200°C/400°F/Gas 6 for 5 minutes.

Meanwhile, wash the artichokes, removing the outer leaves and the inner strings; leave them in water with lemon added, to prevent artichokes from blackening, then cut them into thin slices.

Chop the shallot and the sweet chilli, then quickly brown them in a saucepan with oil. Pour in the artichokes and cook with hot stock on a low heat. When ready, add parsley, half of the cashew nuts and a little grated lemon rind. Season to taste with salt and pepper, then process the mixture. Place this in a sac-à-poche and fill the filo pastry moulds.

Serve filo pastry cases with artichoke paste and garnish with the remaining cashew nuts and chives.

Veal and porcini carpaccio with grilled Savoy cabbage

Serves 4

Carpaccio
380g/13oz lean veal
2 large caps of porcini mushrooms
¼ Savoy cabbage
6 tbsp delicate extra virgin olive oil
½ lemon
chives
thyme
salt and pepper

Preparation time: 20 minutes
Cooking time: 6 minutes
Difficulty: easy
Wine: Dolcetto di Diano d'Alba

Thoroughly clean porcino caps using damp kitchen paper, then dry them.

Cut the veal into thin slices and marinade it with a citronette prepared by mixing lemon juice with salt, pepper and oil, adding finely chopped chives at the end.

Strip the Savoy cabbage leaves off and thoroughly wash them; grill on the barbecue or on a ridged broiler pan and season.

Cut the porcino into thin slices. Alternate Savoy cabbage with porcino slices and season with oil and thyme. Serve the Savoy cabbage millefeuille with veal carpaccio.

Cook's tip - To change this recipe using the same ingredients, you may blanch Savoy cabbage leaves in salted water for 3 minutes then line 4 single portion moulds with these leaves. Dice mushrooms and veal, then combine with 1 boiled and mashed potato and flavour with thyme. Fill the moulds closing them with the overlapping leaves and bake at 190°C/375°F/Gas 5 for 15 minutes.

Green pepper-flavoured sweetbread nests

Serves 4

Pie
500g/1lb 2oz/2 cups sweetbreads
1 yellow pepper
1 red pepper
2 tbsp peanuts
1 tsp green ground pepper
30ml/1fl oz/2 tbsp "passito" wine (made from raisins)
30g/1oz/2 tbsp butter
1 tbsp white vinegar
1 tbsp extra virgin olive oil
thyme
salt and pepper

Potatoes
4 new potatoes
100ml/4fl oz/½ cup thick veal gravy
butter

Preparation time: 25 minutes
Cooking time: 40 minutes
Difficulty: medium
Wine: Alto Adige Terlaner

Clean the sweetbreads, cook them in salted water acidulated with a tablespoon of white vinegar, then cut into small pieces. Heat the butter in a large copper saucepan, chop peanuts using a knife, add them and season with pepper; add sweetbreads and raise the heat. Cook for 4 minutes stirring often then pour in "passito" wine (at room temperature). Add salt and flavour with thyme, then go on cooking until sweetbreads are well done.

Cut peppers into rings (one to fit within another), remove inner pulp and seeds and brush with oil. Cook under the oven grill, being careful to keep their shape.

Using a pasta cutter fill 2 pepper rings (red-yellow) with sweetbreads and arrange the whole on a baking sheet.

Peel the potatoes, cut them into very thin round slices, brush with butter and bake them slightly overlapped. Cook sweetbread nests "au gratin" and serve them together with potatoes and hot veal gravy.

Leek cannolo with caprino cheese and onion sauce

Serves 4

Cannolo
300g/11oz/1½ cups caprino cheese
2 large leeks
2 white onions
extra virgin olive oil

Base
2 red tomatoes
2 bunches of rocket
1 tbsp pine nuts
1 tbsp capers, chopped
extra virgin olive oil
salt and pepper

Preparation time: 25 minutes
Cooking time: 15 minutes
Difficulty: easy
Wine: Greco di Tufo

Remove the green part of the leeks. Cut each leek in 2 parts and shape 4 "cannoli" (horns) gently pulling out the inner part of the leeks, being careful not to break them. Blanch them in water for 30 seconds and leave to cool.

Peel and cut the onions into round slices and cook them in a saucepan with a drizzle of oil until transparent, adding water if necessary. Slightly cool the onions and combine them with the creamy cheese (if the mixture turns out too soft, add some Parmesan cheese and breadcrumbs).

Using a pastry bag, fill the leek "cannoli" and wrap them with clingfilm; allow to rest in the fridge.

Wash tomatoes and rocket, then cut them into small pieces; mix with pine nuts and capers, then season with a drizzle of oil, salt and pepper. Arrange rocket and tomatoes on plates, then complete with cannolo slices.

LEEKS
This vegetable is widely used in cooking; you'd better choose very fresh and withish leeks, because white leeks are more tender and taste less strong. The white part is generally used more in cooking than the green one.

Caprese

Serves 4

Caprese
500g/1lb 2oz/2 cups buffalo mozzarella
500g/1lb 2oz/2 cups fresh tomatoes
4 tbsp extra virgin olive oil
oregano
salt

To garnish
basil

Preparation time: 10 minutes
Difficulty: easy
Wine: Capri Bianco

Wash and wipe the tomatoes, then cut them into rather thick segments; slice the mozzarella cheese too. Arrange tomato segments on a serving plate and cover (or alternate) them with sliced mozzarella. Season with olive oil, a pinch of salt and a generous amount of oregano. Serve the caprese fresh garnished with basil leaves.

Tip - If you prefer, you may use fior di latte mozzarella instead of buffalo mozzarella; fior di latte mozzarella is made from cow's milk.

Fish and shellfish

Sea bass, tuna, salmon, shellfish and
crustaceans are the main ingredients
of delicate and original appetizers.
Start your dinners with
taste and imagination.

Sea bass roll with cockles and vegetables

Serves 4

Roll

4 sea bass fillets (130g/4½oz/1 cup each)
10 fresh cockles
2 cloves of garlic, crushed
1 chilli
2 tbsp extra virgin olive oil
basil
salt and pepper

Vegetables

1 small aubergine
2 courgettes
1 tbsp extra virgin olive oil
oil for deep-frying
thyme
salt

Lentil sauce

60g/2¼oz/¼ cup red lentils
1 fresh red chilli
200ml/7fl oz/1 cup vegetable stock
3 tbsp extra virgin olive oil
salt

Preparation time: 25 minutes
Cooking time: 70 minutes
Difficulty: medium
Wine: Elba Bianco

In a covered saucepan cook cockles together with garlic, chilli and oil on a high heat until the cockles open; season to taste with salt and pepper. Cut sea bass fillets in half; place them between 2 oiled clingfilm sheets and lightly pound using a meat pounder.

Remove cockles from their shells, arrange some in the middle of each fillet, add a basil leaf and roll the fillet up, then wrap it in clingfilm giving it a "candy shape".

Wash and dice the vegetables, then fry them in hot oil; drain on kitchen paper and sauté in a pan with a drizzle of olive oil, thyme and salt.

Overcook the lentils in stock with a small piece of red chilli; process the lentils in a food processor, then pass them through a sieve; season to taste with salt and olive oil.

Steam the fish purses, remove the clingfilm and serve with vegetables and red lentil sauce.

"Catalan style" scampi on a nest of vegetables

Serves 4

"Catalan style" scampi
16 medium-small scampi
2 new carrots
1 cucumber
1 heart of celery

Vinagrette
3 tbsp balsamic vinegar
4 tbsp extra virgin olive oil
salt and white pepper

Court bouillon
1 shallot
1 stick of celery
1 bay leaf
1 carrot
1 stalk of parsley
a dash of white wine
ground black pepper

Preparation time: 15 minutes
Cooking time: 4 minutes
Difficulty: easy
Wine: Collio Tocai Friuliano

Wash the celery and thinly slice it. Peel cucumber and carrots, then cut them into julienne strips (remember to discard the cucumber pips).

Simmer all the ingredients for the court bouillon, then blanch scampi for about 4 minutes. Peel the scampi and serve them in 4 glass bowls on a nest of vegetables.

Dissolve salt in vinegar, pour in oil and gently beat using a little whisk, then add a pinch of white pepper. Season the catalan style scampi and serve.

Cook's tip - If you want to add a more exotic flavour to this recipe, try to add some pineapple slices, some strawberries or some white melon slices. For a much tastier recipe, mix scampi with prawns or lobsters.

Courgette rolls with tuna and capers

Serves 4

Courgette

3 large courgettes
180g/6½oz/1 cup tuna in oil
1 tbsp extra virgin olive oil
8 capers, drained and rinsed
6 green and black olives, stoned
1 spring onion
1 leek, cut into thin strips
salt and pepper

To garnish

5 leaves of fresh basil

Preparation time: 20 minutes
Cooking time: 15 minutes
Difficulty: easy
Wine: Soave Classico

Wash courgettes and cut away their tips, slice them lenghtwise into strips (not too thin) and grill. Put drained tuna and cleaned spring onion in the food processor, add 1 tablespoon of extra virgin olive oil and process all the ingredients.

Combine coarsely chopped olives and capers with the mixture and season to taste with salt and pepper.

Arrange the filling in the middle of the courgette slices and roll them up.

Blanch the leek in salted water for a couple of minutes, close the rolls using leek strips and garnish with basil. Allow the courgette rolls to rest for 30 minutes and serve cold.

Cook's tip - If you prefer a lighter version of this recipe, instead of tuna use 200g/7oz/1 cup of fresh tofu, boiled in hot water for 7 minutes. Follow the above instructions and remember to process tofu with the spring onion, capers and olives to fill the courgettes Stuff the courgettes and you'll get a tasty vegetarian appetizer.

Scallops and porcini mushrooms with calamint

Serves 4

Scallops
4 large scallops in the shell
2 small fresh porcini mushrooms
2 sprigs of calamint, finely chopped
2 tbsp delicate extra virgin olive oil
½ tbsp fine breadcrumbs
white and black pepper
salt

Preparation time: 20 minutes
Cooking time: 1 minutes
Difficulty: easy
Wine: Metodo Classico Franciacorta Brut

Wash the scallops and remove them from their shells, thinly slice them diagonally using a thin-blade knife. Thoroughly clean the shells and set them aside (you may like to use them for serving, instead of dishes).

Thoroughly clean porcini mushrooms with a small knife and discard the earthy bottom of the stems; wipe them with damp kitchen paper. Slice the mushrooms finely and set them aside.

Arrange the scallop slices and porcini mushrooms alternately in the shells.

Season with salt, pepper and a drizzle of extra virgin olive oil. Add the calamint and dust with a pinch of breadcrumbs. Bake the shells under a grill for no longer than 1 minute and serve.

Note - Calamint, also known as pennyroyal, is an herbaceous plant very similar to mint but with a lighter and more delicate fragrance.

Sole rolls with spinach

Serves 4

Rolls

4 soles (250g/9oz each)
100g/3½oz fresh salmon
100g/3½oz/1 cup fresh spinach

Salad

2 bunches of glasswort (or spinach)
1 cucumber
4 red tomatoes

Eggs

8 quail eggs

Anchovy sauce

4 anchovies, preserved in salt
300g/11oz Tuscan bread
6 tbsp extra virgin olive oil
2 tbsp red wine vinegar
salt and pepper

Preparation time: 40 minutes
Cooking time: 15 minutes
Difficulty: medium
Wine: Friuli Isonzo Sauvignon

Skin the soles and fillet them. Flatten the fillets using a meat pounder, then cut the salmon into slices and arrange them on the sole fillets (see photo 1). Wash the spinach leaves, cut away their stalks and arrange over the fillets (see photo 2). Roll the fillets up and allow to rest in the fridge for a couple of minutes. Thoroughly clean the glasswort and blanch in boiling water for 1 minute; drain and leave to cool in cold water.

Boil quail eggs for 1 minute and drop immediately in cold water. Shell the eggs being careful not to damage them. Peel the cucumber and thinly dice it. Peel the tomatoes, remove their pulp and dice them. Cut the bread into 5 mm/¼in thick slices, dice them and arrange on a baking tray with oil, salt, pepper and chopped anchovies; add a little vinegar, oil, pepper and leave to marinade for a couple of minutes. Season sole rolls with oil, salt and pepper then steam them for 3 minutes. Steam the glasswort too; sprinkle it onto plates and lay the rolls over (see photo 3). Pour on the marinaded bread and a drizzle of oil, then serve.

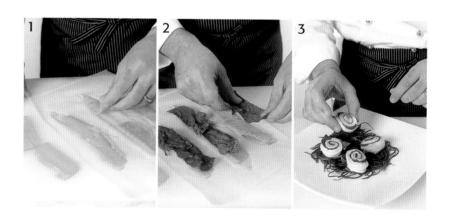

Marinaded salmon on fennel and artichoke salad

Serves 4

Salmon

300g/11oz fresh salmon fillet
1 sprig of dill
3 tbsp extra virgin olive oil
2 fresh spring onions, chopped
2 tsp sugar
1 lemon
white pepper and salt

Salad

2 artichoke hearts
2 fennel bulbs
4 tbsp extra virgin olive oil
1 lemon
salt

Preparation time: 30 minutes
Difficulty: easy
Wine: Metodo Classico Franciacorta Rosé

Discard salmon skin and bones, then flavour the fillet with olive oil, salt, sugar and dill mixture. Allow to rest in the fridge for at least 8 hours, then thoroughly wash the salmon. Squeeze the lemon juice.

Combine spring onions with lemon juice and use this mixture to season the fish. Add white pepper and leave again to rest for at least 8 hours. Wash the salmon again and cut it into thin slices.

Cut artichoke and fennel with a slicing machine or a mandoline slicer, season with extra virgin olive oil, lemon and salt; arrange the serving plate with this salad and serve the fish fillet on it.

Note - Dill is an aromatic herb that facilitates digestion. It blooms late in spring and in summer. Its leaves and inflorescences are used to flavour many dishes, in particular fish, vegetables in oil and soups. Crumble dill with your fingertips or cut it using scissors, in order to keep its taste and aroma unaltered.

Squid with potato sauce and cuttlefish

Serves 4

Squid

52 squid
150g/5½oz/1 cup onion
4 quail eggs, shelled
1 summer truffle
1 tbsp white vinegar
extra virgin olive oil
salt and pepper

Potato sauce

300g/11oz/1½ cup potatoes, cut into pieces
4-5 squid bladders with cuttlefish
100g/3½oz/1 cup leeks, chopped
100ml/3½fl oz/½ cup scampi and red prawn
bisque
300ml/10fl oz/1¼ cups fish fumet
1 sprig of marjoram
extra virgin olive oil
basil
salt and pepper

Preparation time: 30 minutes
Cooking time: 25 minutes
Difficulty: medium
Wine: Bianco d'Alcamo

Clean and wash the squid (see photo 1), dry them and stuff with browned onion. Set squid heads aside.

To prepare the potato sauce, quickly brown the leeks with a drizzle of extra virgin oil (see photo 2), then add potatoes, basil and marjoram. Cook for a couple of minutes, then pour in bisque and fish fumet and cook over a low heat for 15 more minutes. Season with salt and pepper and process the sauce adding a tablespoon of extra virgin oil and cuttlefish. Set aside in a warm place.

Put the squids on a bakling tray, season with a drizzle of oil, salt and pepper, then bake them in a fan oven at 220°C/425°F/Gas 7 for 5 minutes. In a saucepan bring to the boil some lightly salted water, acidulated with a tablespoon of white vinegar. Stir constantly using a wooden spoon, in order to create a sort of whirlpool, then drop quail eggs. As soon as they are cooked on the outside, drain them in cold water. Stir-fry squid heads in a pan with a drizzle of oil. Pour a ladle of potato sauce into 4 soup bowls and arrange in each bowl 13 squid in a ring; in the middle of this ring place 13 heads, a quail egg and ¼ of the squid juices, then season with a drizzle of oil and grated truffle.

Crispy pastries with tuna mousse

Serves 4

Pastries
2 filo pastry sheets
200g/7oz/1 cup tuna in oil
150g/5oz/1 cup haricot beans, precooked
4 tbsp extra virgin olive oil
1 sprig of rosemary
100 ml/3½fl oz/½ cup vegetable stock
1 clove of garlic, crushed
a knob of butter
salt and pepper

Preparation time: 20 minutes
Cooking time: 10 minutes
Difficulty: easy
Wine: Roero Arneis

Cut filo pastry into pieces (about 4cm/1½in square); arrange them on a baking tray lined with greaseproof paper, brush with melted butter and a little salt and pepper. Bake at 190°C/375°F/Gas 5 for about 6 minutes until nicely browned.

Heat the oil in a saucepan with the garlic clove, then add beans and a sprig of rosemary. Soon afterwards remove garlic and rosemary and season to taste with salt and pepper; pour in the stock and cook the beans for 5 more minutes. Put the tuna in a food processor, add 2 tablespoons of beans together with their liquid and a drizzle of oil, then process to a smooth mousse. Set aside. Pour the remaining beans into a blender or food processor and work to get a smooth and rather liquid purée, then pass it through a wide-mesh sieve. Arrange small filo pastries on a plate with tuna mousse in between, then serve with bean purée and a drizzle of oil.

Cook's tip - You can get a much tastier recipe if you use fresh fish instead of tuna in oil. Cut 350g/12oz/1½ cup of fresh tuna into pieces and stir-fry in a non-stick pan with oil, a crushed garlic clove, thyme, salt and pepper. Thinly slice the fish and arrange crispy filo pastries, bean purée and tuna slices alternately on a serving plate.

Scallops and Brussels sprouts with white polenta

Serves 4

Polenta
80g/3oz/¾ cup white maize flour
500ml/18fl oz/2¼ cups fish fumet
1 tbsp salted butter
3 tbsp extra virgin olive oil
1 sprig of thyme
salt and pepper

And
12 small scallops
16 Brussels sprouts
4 shallots
1 sprig of thyme
extra virgin olive oil
salt and pepper

Preparation time: 30 minutes
Cooking time: 45 minutes
Difficulty: easy
Wine: Gambellara

Wrap unpeeled shallots and a sprig of thyme in aluminium foil. Bake in a preheated oven at 200°C/400°F/Gas 6 for about 25 minutes, then leave to slightly cool in the foil. Remove the scallops from their shells, thoroughly clean them, season with a drizzle of oil and keep in the fridge wrapped in clingfilm.

Discard the outer leaves and the hard bottom of Brussels sprouts, then steam them for 6-7 minutes.

Filter the fish fumet, heat it in a heavy-bottomed saucepan and pour in the maize flour. Gently cook stirring constantly and season with thyme, salt, pepper, oil and butter. Leave the polenta rather soft and creamy.

Heat a non-stick pan and briefly stir-fry the scallops, adding salt and pepper only when ready.

Arrange the serving plates with a layer of polenta, then sprouts cut into 4 segments, then another layer of soft polenta. Top with hot scallops and candied shallot.

Small flying squid with peppers and balsamic onions

Serves 4

Flying squid
12 flying squid
½ red pepper
½ yellow pepper
½ green pepper
2 tbsp extra virgin olive oil
spices for grilled fish

Onions
16 borettane onions
2 tbsp extra virgin olive oil
2 tbsp balsamic vinegar
1 tsp sugar

Potatoes
2 new potatoes
2 tbsp extra virgin olive oil
thyme and rosemary
salt and pepper

To garnish
2 tbsp pesto without cheese

Preparation time: 30 minutes
Cooking time: 25 minutes
Difficulty: medium
Wine: Sicilia Chardonnay

Thoroughly wash and gut the flying squid. Cut peppers into strips 2cm/¾in longer than the squid.

Stuff the flying squids with mixed peppers and leave them to marinade in a bowl for 10 minutes with a drizzle of extra virgin olive oil and fish spices. Meanwhile, wash the onions and quickly brown them in a casserole with a little oil and sugar; as soon as candied, pour in the balsamic vinegar, let it reduce, then add a little water and continue cooking until ready.

Place the squid on a small baking tray and bake at 200°C/400°F/Gas 6 for 10 minutes.

Peel and thinly dice the potatoes, stir-fry them in a saucepan over a high heat together with oil, thyme and rosemary; season to taste with salt and pepper.

Arrange potatoes on the plates, lay the flying squid over and complete with onions. Spoon ½ tablespoon of pesto on one side and serve.

Tip - To prepare pesto sauce, put 100g/3½ oz/1 cup of pine nuts, 6 tbsp of oil and ½ garlic clove in a food processor and process all the ingredients; then add some cooking salt, 100g/3½oz/1 cup of basil leaves and process for another few seconds.

Courgette ring with squid

Serves 4

Courgette

7-8 small courgettes with flowers
100g/3½oz/½ cup tiny squid
½ red pepper
½ yellow pepper
6 tbsp extra virgin olive oil
2 slices of soft bread
100ml/3fl oz/½ cup milk
salt

Preparation time: 35 minutes
Cooking time: 20 minutes
Difficulty: medium
Wine: Malvasia Istriana

Roast peppers directly on the heat, then close them in a plastic bag to "sweat" for about 15 minutes so that you can easily peel them. Meanwhile, remove the courgette tips and cut them into thin slices lengthwise using a mandoline slicer or a slicing machine. Steam for a few minutes, then take 4 ring moulds (lightly greased with oil) and line them with upright courgette slices.

Soak bread slices in milk, drain and squeeze well; crumble them in a bowl and season to taste.

Peel peppers and dice them, setting some strips aside to garnish the dish. Combine diced peppers with bread and mix well. Fill the moulds with the bread and pepper mixture and fold the excess courgette slices over the mixture. Turn out the courgette rings and steam heat.

Blanch the tiny squid in salted water and arrange them inside the courgettes rings, which have been steam heated. Garnish with pepper strips and a drizzle of oil. Complete the dish with fried courgette flowers.

COURGETTES

From a nutritional point of view, courgettes are an excellent food: Low in calories but rich in carbohydrates, proteins, mineral salts (phosphorus and iron), vitamin A and vitamin C. Though spring vegetables, courgettes are easily available in any season. You only have to carefully check that their pulp is firm and their skin doesn't have spots or any other imperfections.

Salt cod with peach sauce

Serves 4

Pie

150g/5oz salt cod, drained and rinsed
250g/9oz yellow potatoes, cut into very small slices
1 shallot, chopped
2 tbsp extra virgin olive oil
200ml/7fl oz/¾ cup milk
parsley
salt and pepper

Sauce

2 yellow peaches, diced
½ lemon
a dash of white wine

Preparation time: 30 minutes
Cooking time: 30 minutes
Difficulty: easy
Wine: Alto Adige Sauvignon

Let the shallot cook in a saucepan with 2 tablespoons of oil. Peel the salt cod, discard its bones and place in the saucepan together with potatoes; pour in milk and cook for about 20-30 minutes. Keep some warm water aside to pour in the mixture if this thickens too much. When ready, add parsley and mix all the ingredients using a mixer or a blender. Season to taste. Place salt cod in a pyrex dish and allow to rest in the fridge for 1 hour.

Meanwhile, briefly stir-fry peaches in a non-stick pan, pour in lemon juice and white wine and let it reduce; process the mixture in a food processor.

Using a pasta cutter, cut a circle from the fish mixture, plate it and serve with peach sauce.

Rice millefeuille with salmon, courgettes and aromatic oil

Serves 4

Millefeuille
6 sheets of deep-frozen rice pastry
240g/8½oz smoked salmon
2 courgettes
6 tbsp extra virgin olive oil
1 small bunch of aromatic herbs (thyme, chervil, chives)
oil for deep-frying
salt and pepper

To garnish
100g/3½oz/½ cup ricotta cheese

Preparation time: 25 minutes
Cooking time: 10 minutes
Difficulty: easy
Wine: Friuli Collio Pinot Grigio

Finely chop aromatic herbs and leave to infuse in extra virgin olive oil with salt and pepper. Thaw out the rice pastry sheets and cut them into triangles; fry in hot oil for 10 seconds, turning them only once, then drain on kitchen paper without adding salt.

Thinly slice the salmon and trim these slices the same size as pastry triangles.

Wash courgettes and slice them diagonally using a thin mandoline slicer (or a slicing machine). Shape the millefeuille alternating layers of fried rice triangles, salmon and courgettes. Season each layer with aromatic herb oil and complete with grated ricotta cheese.

Cook's tip - Rice pastry, a product native to China and Japan, is easily available in shops that sell ethnic food and gastronomic specialities. It can be replaced with pasta for wonton or spring rolls. Mix 2 cups of flour and 2 eggs in a bowl, pour in enough water (about 1½ tablespoons) to make a rather firm dough, transfer it onto a floured work top and knead for 5-7 minutes. Cover with a damp cloth and allow to rest for about 20 minutes. Flatten the dough to a very thin sheet using a rolling pin or a pasta maker.

Pepper and octopus rolls with sauce

Serves 4

Rolls

1kg/2lb 4oz/6 cups octopus
4 tbsp extra virgin olive oil
3 red peppers
1 glass of white wine
1 sprig of rosemary
1 bio lemon
1 sprig of marjoram
1 small bunch of parsley
1 tbsp capers, pickled
1 tbsp white vinegar
chilli
salt and pepper

To garnish

100g/3½oz curly endive or lamb's lettuce

Preparation time: 30 minutes
Cooking time: 12 minutes
Difficulty: medium
Wine: Colli del Trasimeno Bianco

Place the octopus in a stock pot with 3 liltres/12 cups of water, the wine, the rosemary and half a lemon. Lightly salt, cover and simmer for about 40 minutes until the octopus is tender. Turn off the heat and leave to rest for 30 minutes.

Peel peppers and cut them into strips (2 cm/¾in long). Keep 100ml/3½fl oz/½ cup of octopus cooking juices and filter them.

Drain the octopus and cut its tentacles into pieces. Roll a pepper strip around each piece and close the rolls with a stick. Heat the oil in a pan and gently fry the rolls for a couple of minutes, then add the vinegar, octopus juices, salt and chilli. Add capers and chopped aromatic herbs.

Serve the rolls with tender curly endive lettuce.

CAPERS
Caper is a fleshy leafed and white flowered shrub that grows wild in the Mediterranean areas, in particular on waste and poor soils. The capers we know and use so much in cooking are the flower buds. They are picked still closed and unripe and can be preserved in salt, pickle or brine.

Artichoke hearts, cod mousse and diced polenta

Serves 4

Artichokes
12 globe artichokes
1 clove garlic
3 tbsp extra virgin olive oil
½ glass of white wine
1 lemon
1 tbsp parsley, chopped
marjoram
salt

Cod
300g/10½oz fresh white cod fillet
1 litre/4 cups milk
1 clove garlic
1 bay leaf
3 tbsp extra virgin olive oil
salt and pepper

Polenta
200g/7oz/1 cup cold polenta
300ml/10fl oz/1¼ oil for deep-frying
salt

Preparation time: 40 minutes
Cooking time: 40 minutes
Difficulty: medium
Wine: Pinot Grigio del Piave

Clean the artichokes discarding the hard outer leaves, cut away the tips and remove inner core using a corer. As soon as they are ready, place them in a bowl with water acidulated with lemon juice.

In a large, shallow casserole heat 3 tablespoons of oil together with a garlic clove and marjoram. Arrange the artichokes (keeping their stalks down), add salt, pour in wine and, once the alcohol has evaporated, cover and let cook for 20-25 minutes. In another casserole bring milk to the boil with a bay leaf, a garlic clove, salt and pepper. Add the cod fillet and cook over low heat for 12-15 minutes. Once done, drain, put in a food processor and process until smooth gradually adding oil. Season to taste with salt and pepper. Cut the polenta into irregular pieces and fry them in hot oil until crisp. Drain on kitchen paper and lightly salt.

Fill the warm heart of each artichoke with a quenelle of cod mousse; lay them on a serving plate together with diced polenta. Filter artichoke juice, add parsley and a drizzle of extra virgin olive oil, then sprinkle this mixture on the dish before serving.

Flaked stockfish with tomatoes and botargo

Serves 4

Stockfish

4 ripe tomatoes
200g/7oz stockfish (previously soaked)
100g/3½oz/½ cup stockfish entrails
6 tbsp extra virgin olive oil
2 courgettes
200ml/7fl oz/¾ cup balsamic vinegar
1 clove garlic, crushed
1 small bunch of parsley
½ lemon
pressed and dried grey mullet roe (botargo)
salt and pepper

Preparation time: 20 minutes
Cooking time: 30 minutes
Difficulty: easy
Wine: Torbato di Alghero

Wash tomatoes and cut off the tops; remove seeds and inner pulp, then salt the tomato inside. Turn them upside down on kitchen paper in order to dry them.

Boil stockfish in plenty of water with lemon and parsley. Drain the fish and set it aside.

Wash courgettes and cut away their tips. Cut the green part into very thin julienne strips and stir-fry in a saucepan together with a drizzle of extra virgin olive oil.

Add extra virgin olive oil and garlic to another pan and quickly cook tomatoes on a high heat.

Fill the tomatoes with courgette strips and season with a drizzle of extra virgin olive oil.

Reduce balsamic vinegar to one fifth. Alternate flaked stockfish and botargo slices over the stuffed tomatoes, then complete the dish with sautéed stockfish entrails and reduced balsamic vinegar.

Spicy seafood sauté

Serves 4

Sauté

250g/9oz/1 cup cockles
200g/7oz/1 cup mussels
250g/9oz/1 cup clams
5 cherry or "plum" tomatoes
2 cloves of garlic
3 tbsp extra virgin olive oil
½ wine glass of dry white wine
1 red chilli, crumbled
4 slices of home-made bread
parsley
salt

Preparation time: 20 minutes
Cooking time: 10 minutes
Difficulty: easy
Wine: Ischia Bianco

Thoroughly wash the seafood in several changes of water, scrubbing clams and removing brown strings of mussels. Purge them in three different bowls with salted water. Meanwhile, wash the tomatoes and cut them into 4 segments; chop the parsley (see photo 1). Heat the oil in a saucepan together with a thinly chopped garlic clove, a chilli and a little parsley. Add cockles, turn up the heat and cook for 3 minutes. Pour in the wine, when the alcohol has evaporated, add mussels and clams. Bring to the boil again, add tomatoes (see photo 2) and the remaining parsley, cover and cook until the seafood shells open.

Toast the sliced bread, rub with a little garlic (see photo 3); arrange them on serving plates, pour over hot sauté and serve.

Note - A purging process is useful to eliminate sand from the inside of molluscs; simply washing them can't get this result. Soaking them in water, with a proper addition of salt, makes molluscs "breathe", allowing them to give off sand.

Tuna and swordfish with fennel

Serves 4

Tuna and swordfish
220g/7oz/1 cup fresh tuna pulp
220g/7oz swordfish
1 juicy lemon
extra virgin olive oil
wild fennel, chopped
salt and pepper

Parsley flan
1 bunch of parsley
1 egg
2 tbsp breadcrumbs
1 tbsp fresh cream
1 tbsp cornflour

To garnish
2 tbsp black olive purée
1 red tomato
extra virgin olive oil

Preparation time: 35 minutes
Cooking time: 25 minutes
Difficulty: easy
Wine: Metodo Trento Talento Extra Brut

Thinly dice the fish (about 5mm/¼in square) then place it in a bowl; season to taste with oil, lemon, a little salt, pepper and fennel.

Put the fish into 4 round moulds (pasta cutters), cover with clingfilm and put a glass of water on the top of each mould to press them down; keep in the fridge for 2 hours.

Blanch parsley in salted water for 2 minutes (to take its bitter taste away). Squeeze well and weigh about 200g/7oz/1 cup of parsley, then process with egg yolk and cream in a food processor. Add breadcrumbs and leave to rest for 5 minutes.

Beat egg white until stiff and gently mix it with the parsley sauce, add sifted cornflour too and pour the mixture into small aluminium moulds, lightly greased with butter. Bake at 180°C/350°F/Gas 4 for about 20 minutes. Wash and dice the tomato, then season it.

Serve the fish with a parsley flan cut in half, and a tablespoon of tomato. Complete with black olive purée and a drizzle of olive oil.

Salmon trout and smoked sturgeon roll with potatoes

Serves 4

Roll
2 salmon trout fillets
200g/7oz smoked sturgeon, sliced
6 tbsp delicate extra virgin olive oil
poppy seeds
thyme, chopped
pepper

Potatoes
2 potatoes
1 sachet of powdered saffron
100ml/3½fl oz/½ cup vegetable stock
1 red pepper
a small piece of Savoy cabbage
salt

To garnish
1 tbsp pine nuts
2 red tomatoes
sunflower oil
basil
salt and pepper

Preparation time: 35 minutes
Cooking time: 40 minutes
Difficulty: medium
Wine: Lugana

Gently bone trout fillets and open them using a knife with a thin, elastic blade. Season with thyme and pepper, then fill them with lightly overlapped sturgeon slices.

Wash the pepper, cut it into regular strips and set the remaining part aside. Heat a little oil in a saucepan and stir-fry pepper strips until nicely browned, then arrange some in the middle of each trout fillet. Roll the fillets up, wrap in clingfilm and close them in the shape of a "sweet". Steam for 7 minutes, then let them slightly cool. Meanwhile, peel the potatoes and, using a corer, get 16 small balls out of them; boil in vegetable stock with saffron and salt. Prepare a mirepoix with Savoy cabbage and the remaining pepper, roasted in a non-stick pan without oil. As soon as potato balls are done, drain and roll them in the mirepoix. Blanch tomatoes and cool them in water and ice; gently peel them and fry their skins in oil.

Spread poppy seeds on the roll and cut it into thick slices. Serve with potato balls, fried skins of tomatoes and a light pesto prepared by processing basil, pine nuts, salt, oil and pepper.

Prawns in brandy sauce

Serves 4

Prawns

600g/1lb 4oz/3 cups king prawns
1 shallot, chopped
1 wine glass of white wine
2 ripe tomatoes
½ wine glass of brandy
100ml/3½fl oz/½ cup fresh single cream
2 tbsp extra virgin olive oil
parsley, chopped
salt and pepper

Preparation time: 15 minutes
Cooking time: 15 minutes
Difficulty: easy
Wine: Metodo Classico Franciacorta,
zero dosage

Blanch tomatoes in boiling water for 30 seconds, peel and coarsely cut them coarsely. Gently brown the shallot in a saucepan with oil and 2 or 3 spoonfuls of water.

Add king prawns and leave them to cook for a couple of minutes. Sprinkle with brandy, let the alcohol evaporate then pour in the white wine and let it reduce to half.

Add tomato pieces, salt and pepper and cook for about 10 minutes. Drain prawns and set them aside. Combine cream with liquor and let this mixture reduce on a high heat.

Season to taste with salt and pepper, dust with parsley and serve prawns together with brandy sauce.

Cook's tip - You may turn this hors d'oeuvre into a tasty main course by simply serving prawns with a small timbale of boiled Basmati rice.

Oysters with "black" oil and citron

Serves 4

Oysters
8 oysters
150g/5oz/1 cup black olives
6 tbsp extra virgin olive oil
1 citron (or lemon)
white pepper

Preparation time: 10 minutes
Cooking time: 2 hours
Difficulty: easy
Wine: Metodo Classico Franciacorta
Extra Brut

Wash, wipe and stone the olives. Cut into 2 parts, arrange on a baking sheet (preferably with holes) and let them dry in the oven at 70-80°C/160°F-175°F for about 2 hours, then leave to cool.

Put the olives into a food mixer with oil and a little pepper, then process until the oil turns black. Pass it through a fine-mesh sieve and collect in a bowl.

Open the oysters on bed of ice, lightly sprinkle with some drops of citron juice and a pinch of grated peel. Add a drizzle of "black" oil and serve immediately.

Cook's tip - If you don't like the taste of raw oysters, serve them with a filling made of flavoured breadcrumbs. Quickly brown a garlic clove in a saucepan with oil and parsley, add breadcrumbs and season to taste with salt and pepper. Open the oysters, cover them with this mixture and bake under an oven grill at max heat for a couple of minutes.

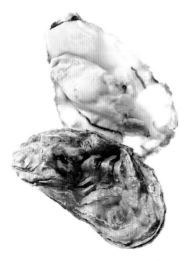

OYSTERS
The best way to prepare oysters is to open them just at the moment you want to eat them using an oyster knife (with a short and thick blade and provided with a hand guard): place the knife tip in the crenulate margin, taking care to protect the hand that holds the oyster by covering it with a folded towel or with a proper glove.

Small "turbans" of steamed sole and prawns

Serves 4

Turbans

2 fresh soles
8 prawn tails
1 orange
1 spring onion
6 tbsp extra virgin olive oil
2 potatoes
cuttlefish ink
oil for deep-frying
1 small bunch of parsley
red pepper
salt

Preparation time: 35 minutes
Cooking time: 25 minutes
Difficulty: easy
Wine: Sorni Bianco

Cut eight fillets from the soles and shell the prawns. Place a prawn on each fillet with the tail overhanging the edge of the sole. Roll up the fillet so that the prawn tail sticks up from the center of the roll. Steam the rolls in a vegetable steamer.

Peel the potatoes, thinly cut them into julienne strips; wash in several changes of water and put half of them into a bowl with cuttlefish ink and a little water.

Squeeze the orange into a pressure cooker with a little water and the parsley. Bring to the boil and place the steamer over; cover and let steam for about 8 minutes.

Fry potato strips in hot oil and salt them. Meanwhile, mix the olive oil with red pepper, salt and some chopped spring onion (the central green-white part). Serve the small "turbans" warm with "citronette" and potato strips.

Norwegian flan

Serves 4

Dough

300g/11oz/2 cups plain white flour
150ml/5fl oz/²/₃ cup lukewarm water
½ block of Brewer's yeast
2 tbsp extra virgin olive oil
salt

Stuffing

200g/7oz salmon
1 potato
3 courgettes, cut into round slices
1 bunch of Swiss chard
6 tbsp extra virgin olive oil
thyme
salt and white pepper

Preparation time: 20 minutes
Cooking time: 40 minutes
Difficulty: easy
Wine: Alto Adige Gewürztraminer

Dissolve the Brewer's yeast in lukewarm water with salt and oil; pour the flour into a pile, make a well in the middle and add dissolved yeast; knead the dough with your fingertips until elastic, then allow to rest under a cloth.

Boil the potato, courgettes and Swiss chard separately in salted water. Butter and flour a mould and line it with rolled dough; prick dough base with a fork.

Layer swiss chard on the pastry and add a drizzle of oil and pepper; make a second layer with sliced potatoes and season again.

Top the surface with thin slices of salmon. Garnish with round courgette slices and season with salt, thyme and oil. Bake at 190°C/375°F/Gas 5 for 40 minutes. Serve cold.

Scallops au gratin with lemon thyme

Serves 4

Pastry

4 large scallops
6 small scallops
8 tbsp breadcrumbs
2 early courgettes, cut into round slices
1 sprig of lemon thyme
2 cloves of garlic
4 tbsp extra virgin olive oil
salt and pepper

Preparation time: 15 minutes
Cooking time: 5 minutes
Difficulty: easy
Wine: Terre di Franciacorta Bianco

In a non-stick pan heat oil with unpeeled garlic, let it become flavoured, then remove the garlic and add breadcrumbs. Toast for a couple of minutes, pour the mixture onto a cold dish adding lemon thyme.

In another pan stir-fry courgettes, season with salt and pepper and leave to slightly cool.

Wash the scallops and remove the thin black thread. Wash the shells and reassemble the molluscs. Place some courgettes on the scallops and spread with breadcrumbs.

Bake the scallops under the oven, grill at the highest temperature for 5 minutes. Serve with a drizzle of oil.

Tip - "Gratin" is a rather "aggressive" and risky cooking method because it can spoil the dish; if it is not correctly done, food could turn out baked unevenly. For this reason you should protect food from direct heat with a breadcrumb layer.

LEMON THYME

It's quite similar to wild thyme, even if it differs in its peculiar lemon flavour. Lemon thyme goes well with fish, eggs and lamb.

Salmon and escarole mousse

Serves 4

Salmon

400g/14oz salmon
60g/2¼oz/¼ cup black olives, stoned
30g/1oz/2tbsp capers, preserved in salt
40g/1½oz/3 tbsp butter
1 head of escarole
4 tbsp mayonnaise
1 shallot, chopped
1 chilli
4 tbsp dry white wine
salt and pepper

To garnish

4 black olives
1 fillet of red pepper in oil
1 baguette

Preparation time: 25 minutes
Cooking time: 10 minutes
Difficulty: easy
Wine: Orvieto Classico

Melt butter in a saucepan with shallot and chilli; wash and coarsely chop escarole and add it. Cover and cook for 5 minutes, until escarole is reduced (in volume); add salmon, pour in wine and let it evaporate. Add olives and capers and finish cooking.

Let cool, then put the mixture into a food processor, adding mayonnaise, salt and pepper. Process until you get a purée then fill a latex mould; place in the fridge for 2 hours. Garnish with olives and red pepper; serve with a slice of toast.

Note - Escarole is used in this recipe because it makes the mousse softer and it doesn't lose consistency during cooking. Moreover, the bitter taste of this vegetable makes a pleasant contrast with the sweet taste of the other ingredients.

Roasted peppers, anchovy and bread rolls

Serves 4

Pepper
1 red pepper
1 yellow pepper
12 anchovy fillets in oil
3 tbsp breadcrumbs
3 tbsp extra virgin olive oil
1 garlic of clove
5 capers, drained and rinsed
parsley, chopped
salt and pepper

Preparation time: 15 minutes
Cooking time: 15 minutes
Difficulty: easy
Wine: Colli di Conegliano Verdiso

Wash the peppers and cut them in half so that you can easily discard their seeds and pith. Bake them in a warm oven under the grill or directly on the heat, turning often until their skin is lightly browned. Close the peppers in a plastic bag to "sweat"; as soon as tepid, peel them and cut into strips.

Cut the garlic in two pieces and quickly brown it in a saucepan with oil, then add chopped capers and breadcrumbs.

Cook on a low heat turning often. Add parsley, salt and pepper. Remove the garlic and drain anchovy fillets.

Arrange 1 anchovy fillet on each pepper strip, dust with toasted breadcrumbs and roll up; close the rolls using a toothpick, then bake in oven at 200°C/400°F/Gas 6 for 4 minutes.

Note - Another way to cook and peel peppers, making them more digestible and versatile in cooking, consists in frying peppers in a small saucepan with hot vegetable oil. Oil temperature shouldn't be too high and gently fry the peppers, so that they can simmer slowly.

Romano Rossi
Il Testamento del Porco

Alessandra Buriani
Buriani

Paolo Teverini
Paolo Teverini

Ezio Santin
Osteria del Ponte

Carla Aradelli
Riva

Marcello e Gianluca Leoni
Il Sole

Top chefs

Chefs from the best Italian
restaurants open their kitchens
to reveal the secrets
of the recipes that made
them famous.

Squid with culatello flavoured turbot on a sweet corn sauce

MARCELLO E GIANLUCA LEONI
Ristorante "Il Sole", Trebbo di Reno (BO)

"New solutions. Juxtapositions and contrasts.
Tradition and groundwork. Ethnic food.
New and unusual shapes and perceptions
on the palate. A cuisine that seeks and propo-
ses. A cuisine that goes beyond ingredients,
mixing, shaping and recreating them".

Pour a drizzle of oil and the leeks into a non-stick pan and
brown quickly. Add turbot flesh, salt and pepper and cook for
a couple of minutes. When ready, put this mixture in a food
processor adding culatello and Parmesan cheese. Process and
use this mixture to fill the squid.

To prepare the sweet corn sauce, boil fresh sweet corn in
salted water. Drain and process with a little beef stock. Pass
through a sieve and leave to dry in a non-stick pan. Season
to taste with salt and pepper. Sauté the squid with a drizzle
of oil and a little chilli. Cut the green part of the courgette
into julienne strips. Place 1 tablespoon of sweet corn purée
in the middle of a plate. Arrange over some stuffed squid and
garnish with courgette julienne (seasoned with oil, salt and
pepper), tomato pulp and a drizzle of balsamic vinegar.

Serves 4

Squid
100g/3½oz/½ cup turbot pulp, diced
20g/¾oz/1 tbsp leeks, chopped
50g/2oz/¼ cup culatello of Zibello, chopped
(or Parma ham)
1 tbsp Parmesan cheese, grated
60 squid, cleaned
extra virgin olive oil
chilli
salt and pepper

Sweet corn sauce
150g/5oz/1 cup fresh sweet corn
beef stock
salt and pepper

To garnish
1 courgette
balsamic vinegar
4 cherry tomatoes

Preparation time: 20 minutes
Cooking time: 20 minutes
Difficulty: easy
Wine: Malvasia Istriana

Spiny lobster slices with warm foie gras

EZIO SANTIN
"Antica Osteria del Ponte" restaurant,
Cassinetta di Lugagnano (MI)

"I'm greedy and curious, I dont' have a hearty appetite and I like tasting food. My ideal lunch begins with crustaceans prepared in any way, raw or sautéed in a pan, with a slice of Piacenza salami or aged coppa."

Simmer spiny lobsters in stock flavoured with vegetables, white wine, finely chopped herbs and pepper corns. Prepare the sauce boiling down vinegar in a saucepan and, when reduced by a quarto, pour in the Port and boil it down again to a quarto adding cooking salt. In another pan reduce balsamic vinegar and cooked must until halved, then combine the two mixtures. Thoroughly mix and add the "colatura di alici", a grind of fresh black pepper and olive oil. Stir the sauce until you get a smooth cream. Cook green beans in salted water until just done and cool them at once in a bowl with water and ice, to keep their bright colour. Peel the lobsters, cut them into slices (lobsters should be warm or at least tepid) and arrange horizontally on a plate. Lightly oil a non-stick saucepan and heat it for a couple of minutes, then sauté the foie gras. Place the foie gras on the spiny lobster, season it with cooking salt and a handful of ground pepper. Sprinkle some thin mango or melon mustard, add green beans, seasoned with a little oil, salt and pepper. Complete with a drizzle of Port sauce and serve.

Serves 4

Lobster
2 spiny lobsters (600g/1lb 5oz each)
3 liltres/12 cups court-bouillon
4 slices of raw goose foie gras
(about 3 tbsp each)
fruit mustard - mango or melon
fine green beans
extra virgin olive oil
salt and mixed pepper

Sauce
100ml/3½fl oz/½ cup apple
or rice vinegar
500ml/18fl oz/2¼ cups red Port
1 tbsp cooking salt
100ml/3½fl oz/½ cup balsamic vinegar
100ml/3½fl oz/½ cup cooked must (sapa)
3 tbsp "colatura di alici" (anchovy garum sauce)
200ml/6½fl oz/¾ cup extra virgin olive oil
fresh black pepper

Preparation time: 15 minutes
Cooking time: 50 minutes
Difficulty: medium
Wine: Metodo Classico Franciacorta
(zero dosage)

Prawns with salami, melon and yoghurt

ALESSANDRA BURIANI
"Buriani" restaurant since 1967,
Pieve di Cento (BO)

"Presentation, or the art of serving a
dish, is an important aspect, however it
must not compromise the substance.
The greatest disappointment is when,
going out for dinner, you choose
a very well presented dish whose taste,
at the end, does not come up to your
expectations."

Serves 4

Prawns
20 prawns
1 small melon
1 "salama da sugo", cooked
mixed salad leaves
aromatic herbs
extra virgin olive oil
salt and pepper

Sauce
2 tbsp natural yoghurt
1 piece of fresh ginger, grated
extra virgin olive oil
salt and pepper

Preparation time: 30 minutes
Cooking time: 10 minutes
Difficulty: easy
Wine: Metodo Classico Franciacorta Saten

Cut the melon and the "salama da sugo" into julienne strips.
Dust the prawns with aromatic herbs, steam them and then
season with extra virgin olive oil, salt and pepper.

Wash the mixed salad leaves and gently dry them. Mix yoghurt
with a drizzle of olive oil, salt, pepper and ginger.

Using a pasta cutter, arrange seasoned salad, prawns,
"salama da sugo" and melon on the plate.

Complete by seasoning with the yoghurt sauce.

Note - "Salama da sugo" is a typical salami from Ferrara,
known since the 15th century, also called the "salamina".
When not available, it can be substituted with standard salami.

French toast with vegetables and cheese

CARLA ARADELLI
"Riva" restaurant, Ponte sull'Olio (PC)

"I like to think of my cooking as something I create free from any restrictions, a cuisine that doesn't follow any patterns but at the same time is able to give pleasant sensations to the palate."

In a mortar, crush pine nuts and basil. Add oil, ricotta cheese, caprino cheese, salt and pepper. Keep the mousse in a cool place.

Cut the bread into 0.5cm/¼in thick slices, soak them in milk and then in a batter prepared with eggs, Parmesan cheese, salt and pepper. Fry the slices in a saucepan with 2 tablespoons of melted butter.

Lightly cook the asparagus and blanch mangetouts together with peas. Cut all the vegetables into julienne strips, discarding the white part from the courgettes, then sauté in oil and salt.

Present the dish creating a frame with vegetables then, over this frame, arrange the mousse and a slice of toast, cut into small strips.

Serves 8

Mousse
2 tbsp extra virgin olive oil
½ tbsp pine nuts
3 basil leaves
150g/5oz/1 cup ricotta cheese
100g/3½oz/½ cup fresh caprino cheese
(Italian goats cheese)
salt and pepper

Toasts
300g/11oz sliced loaf
100 ml/3½fl oz/½ cup milk
2 eggs
2 tbsp Parmesan cheese, grated
60g/2¼oz/¼ cup butter
salt and pepper

Vegetables
40g/1½oz/3 tbsp courgettes
60g/2¼oz/¼ cup spring onions
4 asparagus pears
120g/4oz/1 cup mangetout
45g/1½oz/3 tbsp peas
3 tbsp extra virgin olive oil
salt and pepper

Preparation time: 15 minutes
Cooking time: 5 minutes
Difficulty: easy
Wine: Gutturnio Vivace

Puff pastry with porcini mushrooms and garlicky bacon

ROMANO ROSSI
"Il Testamento del Porco"
restaurant, Ferrara

"To me, service is more important than special effects. Even a mixed selection of salami with home-made bread served unexpectedly while guests wait for their dishes can impress."

Serves 4

Puff pastry
400g/14oz puff pastry
16 slices of bacon
4 medium porcini mushrooms
1 shallot
1 clove garlic
2 tbsp bechamel
1 tbsp extra virgin olive oil
½ wine glass of dry white wine
1 small bunch of parsley, chopped
salt and pepper

Preparation time: 20 minutes
Cooking time: 15 minutes
Difficulty: easy
Wine: Alto Adige Santa Maddalena

Lightly salt the puff pastry, cut it into squares (8-10cm/3¼-4in per side) and bake at about 220°C/425°F/Gas 7 until nicely browned.

Peel and finely chop the shallot and garlic, then sauté in a saucepan with oil. Discard the earthy bottom of the mushroom stems, thoroughly wash and thinly slice mushrooms, then combine with the shallot-garlic mixture.

Pour in dry white wine, let it evaporate, then finish cooking (if too dry, pour in some vegetable stock). Season to taste with salt and pepper, then add the bechamel.

Present the dish layering a puff pastry square and a tablespoon of mushrooms with 2 slices of bacon, baked in a microwave oven at max power for 10 seconds (to make it crispy). Repeat this arrangement and complete with puff pastry and mushrooms. Dust with a pinch of parsley and serve.

Sardines of Cesenatico marinaded with rhubarb and caviar

PAOLO TEVERINI
*"Paolo Teverini" restaurant,
Bagno di Romagna (FC)*

Paolo Teverini bases his cuisine on rules, even
if "the most exciting rule is to break every pattern,
to recreate new and even better ones thanks
to perfect knowledge."

Serves 4

Sardines
16 fresh sardines
200g/7oz/1 cup fresh rhubarb
4 ripe tomatoes
2 tbsp extra virgin olive oil
salt and pepper

To garnish
3 tbsp caviar
aromatic mixed salad

Preparation time: 30 minutes
Cooking time: 10 minutes
Difficulty: easy
Wine: Bianco d'Alcamo

Wash the rhubarb and pass it through a juice extractor to get
its juice. Thoroughly clean the sardines, removing their heads
and their guts, then separate fillets from bones. Salt the fillets
and leave to marinade for 10 minutes in the rhubarb juice.

Wash and peel the tomatoes then, cut them into thick slices.

Pour 1 tablespoon of oil into a non-stick pan and, when hot,
grill tomato slices for a couple of minutes.

Clean and wash the salad, season with the remaining oil,
salt and pepper.

On each plate arrange the sardine fillets, a cooled tomato
slice, salad and caviar. Pour rhubarb juice on the fillets
before serving.

The chef's utensils

A FEW, SIMPLE, STURDY AND EXTREMELY IMPORTANT UTENSILS TO PREPARE DELICIOUS
AND ATTRACTIVE APPETIZERS. A MUST IN THE KITCHEN.

1 **"Grana" knife** - A sturdy steel knife to scoop out chunks of grana cheese. After all, isn't Parmesan the simplest, but also the most delicious appetizer?

2 **Flat whisk** - This unusual shape has been designed to mix small quantities. Perfect to whisk vinaigrette, liquid sauces, creams, but also fluffy omelettes.

3 **Big wheel cutter** - Traditional pizza cutter; cuts even the crunchiest pizza perfectly.

4 **Grater and slicer** - A light, colourful and tasty salad is usually thinly cut in many different shapes. These special graters can be used to julienne carrots or grate hard cheese to prepare simple, but delicious salads.

5 **Beater** - This special small and round steel-wire beater is essential to get rid of lumps in liquids prepared in narrow bowls.

6 **Serving tongs** - Easy-to-grip "scissors" shape. Olives, vol-au-vent and canapés will no longer be dropped...

7 **Round corer** - If you want your appetizers to taste good, but also look nice, you need the right utensils. A round corer creates perfectly shaped fruit or vegetable balls.

Glossary

Agar agar
A product of some types of algae imported from the East. Sometimes it's also used in medicine, while in cuisine it turns out to be very useful as a thickener or substitute for animal gelatin. Agar agar is available in bars, in flakes or in powdered form.

Alga Kombu
A brown alga rich in minerals. If mixed with legumes, it makes them more tender and facilitates their digestion.

Alga Nori
A red alga, also known as sea lettuce. It's available in dried sheets, obtained from pulped alga poured in square moulds, arranged over bamboo mats, then sun dried or baked in large ovens.

Bisque
A French term for crustacean purée (usually made with crayfish shrimps, lobsters, scampi etc). There are different recipes, which is why bisque is prepared using many extra ingredients.

Brick pastry
A very light puff pastry used in Arabic and North-African cuisine. You may fill it with herbs, meat, eggs and tuna or use it for preparing desserts. You can also substitute brick pastry with traditional puff pastry, being careful to stretch it until very thin to make it even lighter.

Concassé
A slicing technique particularly used for vegetables. It consists of cutting vegetables into small and regular cubes (about 5 mm/¼in square).

Court-bouillon
Lightly acidulous liquid, flavoured with vegetables, aromatic herbs and spices. It's often used to simmer fishes.

Filletting
A technique that consists of cutting fish fillets from the middle and side bones and separating one fillet from the other. This can be done by the fishmonger. To fillet a fish, the fishmonger needs a sharp knife with a thin and flexible blade.

Fumet (from fish)
This term refers to a fish stock prepared with what is discarded from a fish (head, bone, scrap) and water, onion, leek, butter and pepper. Just briefly cook it on a low heat from 20 to about 40 minutes.

"Gomasio" (sesame salt)

A seasoning made with sesame seeds and salt, toasted and ground in a mortar. It's used instead of salt to season salads and cooked vegetables.

Lemon thyme

A particular kind of thyme that differs from the well-known "wild thyme" in the delicacy of its taste and in its lightly citrus-flavoured aroma. Lemon thyme is used to season salads and other vegetable dishes.

Marinade

Used for both keeping and soaking foods. A classic marinade is prepared with wine (both white and red), vinegar and oil plus vegetables and aromatic herbs, such as onion, carrots, shallot, bay, juniper berries and cloves.

Mirepoix

Mirepoix, a typical jargon term of haute cuisine, refers to a vegetable mixture used for many dishes. The classic recipe consists of chopped onion, carrot and celery quickly browned in a little butter.

Pasta cutter

This cutter comes in various shapes and dimensions, often made of steel, invented to cut home-made pasta. Besides cutting, you can use these moulds (without the bottoms) to make a shape peculiar to the dish.

Quenelle

A French term that indicates a particular kind of rissole with a lightly lengthened shape, made with the most various ingredients and shaped using hands or the inside of two spoons.

Rice vinegar

Made by alcoholic fermentation of rice flours and subsequent acetic fermentation. Rice vinegar is used to season salads.

Sac-à-poche (pastry bag)

A plastic or cloth cone usually filled with sauces and mixtures to garnish culinary creations with a little bit of imagination.

Tahin

A sauce made with ground sesame seeds used in Middle-Eastern and Greek cuisine as an appetizer. It is usually kept in tins and it is available in specialist shops and in the best supermarkets.

Index

Puff pastry with porcini mushrooms
and garlicky bacon, *134*

R

Rabbit and peppers, *42*
Ravioli of pepper jelly and marinaded avocado, *38*
Rice millefeuille with salmon, courgettes
and aromatic oil, *96*
Ricotta cheese purses with diced tomatoes, *44*
Ricotta cheese sauce with ginger and chives, *12*
Roasted peppers, anchovy and bread rolls, *122*

S

Salmon and escarole mousse, *120*
Salmon sauce, *12*
Salmon trout and smoked sturgeon roll
with potatoes, *108*
Salt cod with peach sauce, *94*
Sardines of Cesenatico marinaded with rhubarb
and caviar, *136*
Savoury pastry rolls (basic dough), *11*
Scallops and Brussels sprouts
with white polenta, *88*
Scallops and porcini mushrooms with calamint, *78*
Scallops au gratin with lemon thyme, *118*
Sea bass roll with cockles and vegetables, *72*
Small flying squid with peppers and balsamic
onions, *90*
Small "turbans" of steamed sole and prawns, *114*

Soft-boiled egg with green sauce, *48*
Sole rolls with spinach, *80*
Spicy lentil pâté, *34*
Spicy seafood sauté, *104*
Spiny lobster slices with warm foie gras, *128*
Spring onions with "cirighin" sauce, *24*
Squid with culatello flavoured turbot
on a sweet corn sauce, *126*
Squid with potato sauce and cuttlefish, *84*
Steamed vegetables with yoghurt mayonnaise, *56*

T

Tarte tatin with courgettes and pecorino cheese, *28*
Tortillas with pepper and maize puddings, *40*
Tricolour vegetable jelly, *36*
Truffled mushrom pâté, *54*
Tuna and swordfish with fennel, *104*

V

Veal and porcini carpaccio with grilled Savoy
cabbage, *62*
Vegetable sushi, *22*

W

Warm sea hors d'oeuvre, *120*
Whisked mustard, *13*

Y

Yoghurt sauce, *12*